RECLAIMING LOVE

A comprehensive guide for Indian families regarding legalised second marriage and getting into togetherness and love

SB VISWANATH

Made with ❤ on the Notion Press Platform

www.notionpress.com

Disclaimer

The content of this book is for general guidance only and should not be considered legal advice. The author is not a licensed attorney, and this book does not constitute legal counsel. Before pursuing a legalised second marriage, readers must consult with a qualified legal professional to understand their specific rights and obligations under applicable laws and regulations. The author and publisher disclaim any liability for any adverse consequences resulting from reliance on the information presented in this book.

Contents

Foreword

"Reclaiming Love" is a profound guide penned by a seasoned lawyer who has witnessed countless tales of heartbreak and resilience. In these pages, the author offers invaluable steps for navigating the complexities of legalised second marriages with wisdom and grace. As you embark on this journey, remember the words of Maya Angelou, "Have enough courage to trust love one more time and always one more time." This book is a testament to the power of love's redemption and the human spirit's capacity to heal and thrive. Embrace each chapter as a beacon of hope, guiding you towards a fulfilling and joyous union.

T.A. Omprakash
Advocate, Trichy,
Tamil Nadu

Summary

The book "Reclaiming Love: A Comprehensive Guide for Indian Families Regarding legalised second marriages" provides a comprehensive guide for couples navigating the unique challenges and opportunities of legalised second marriage in full summary. It covers various aspects of building and sustaining a successful relationship from emotional and practical perspectives.

Embracing changes emphasizes the importance of letting go of past baggage, acknowledging and releasing past hurts and disappointments, and approaching the new marriage with optimism and authenticity. Cultivating self-love and embracing new beginnings are key themes, helping couples start afresh with a positive outlook.

Communication & Connection focuses on building trust and transparency through open and honest communication. It highlights effective communication strategies, such as active listening and empathetic communication, to ensure that partners can share their fears, hopes, and dreams. This chapter also delves into cultivating emotional intimacy and fostering a strong foundation of trust and understanding.

Blending Families addresses the complexities of creating a unified family vision. It explores establishing shared values and goals, creating family rituals and traditions, and navigating parenting challenges. The chapter provides practical strategies for fostering bonds with stepchildren, resolving conflicts related to parenting, and building rapport and trust within the blended family.

Understanding Relationship Dynamics delves into the psychological aspects of relationships, such as exploring attachment styles and their influence on relationship dynamics. It offers guidance on managing conflict constructively, developing conflict resolution skills, and strengthening emotional resilience to support each other through difficult times.

Financial Fusion tackles the challenges of merging finances in a legalised second marriage. It covers assessing individual financial situations, creating joint financial plans, and planning for long-term financial security. This chapter also addresses overcoming money conflicts by resolving differences in financial priorities and spending habits and communicating openly about money.

Cultivating Mutual Growth emphasizes the importance of supporting each other's personal and professional development. It encourages continuous learning, setting shared goals and dreams, and sustaining passion and romance through nurturing intimacy and connection.

Navigating Marriage Laws and Customs explores the legal and cultural aspects of marriage. It covers understanding Hindu, Christian, and Muslim marriage laws, familiarizing them with legal requirements and rituals, and comprehending the rights and responsibilities of spouses under different religious and cultural frameworks.

Blending Families and Cultures revisits the theme of creating a unified family vision and establishing shared values for the blended family. It also addresses navigating parenting challenges, fostering bonds with stepchildren, and creating traditions to bond as a family unit.

Understanding Relationship Dynamics is explored again, focusing on attachment styles, conflict management, and emotional resilience, ensuring a deep understanding of relationship psychology and practical conflict resolution.

Parenting Together provides guidance on co-parenting with ex-partners, maintaining consistency across households, supporting your partner in co-parenting, and addressing loyalty conflicts in children.

Health and Wellness in Blended Families focuses on prioritizing physical health, promoting mental and emotional wellness, building a supportive environment, and navigating healthcare needs for all family members.

Spirituality and Shared Beliefs explores discussing and respecting diverse spiritual beliefs, creating family rituals and traditions, supporting each other's spiritual journeys, and integrating spirituality into family life through shared practices and volunteer activities.

Lifelong Learning and Development emphasizes encouraging continuous learning, supporting career and personal development, cultivating new skills and hobbies, and embracing change and adaptability to prepare for life transitions and maintain a growth mindset.

This summary captures the essence of each chapter, providing a roadmap for couples in legalised second marriages to build strong, resilient, and fulfilling relationships.

With lots of love

SB Viswanath

Introduction

"Love is composed of a single soul inhabiting two bodies."

– Aristotle

In the intricate dance of love, second chances often emerge as a testament to resilience, growth, and the unwavering human capacity for renewal. Just as a skilled conductor orchestrates harmony within a symphony, navigating the complexities of a legalised second marriage requires a delicate balance of art and science.

Proverbs from around the world echo the wisdom gleaned from the tumultuous journey of love:

"Fall seven times, stand up eight." - Japanese Proverb

"Experience is the comb that life gives you after you've lost your hair." - Judith Stern

"A smooth sea never made a skillful sailor." - English Proverb

Love, with its ebbs and flows, its highs and lows, serves as the cornerstone of our existence. It is a force that transcends time and space, binding souls together in a tapestry of shared experiences, emotions, and aspirations. It is in the embrace of love that we find solace, strength, and the courage to embark on new beginnings.

Indeed, the path to a successful legalised second marriage is paved with the lessons learned from past experiences and the willingness to embrace the unknown with open hearts and minds.

As we embark on this exploration of love, commitment, and resilience, let us draw inspiration from the words of the great poet Rumi, who once said, "The wound is the place where the light enters you." May this journey illuminate the hidden corners of our souls, guiding us toward the harmonious union we seek in our second chance at love.

Preface

In the intricate tapestry of life, relationships often weave patterns of joy, challenge, growth, and transformation. For many, the journey of love and partnership leads to the profound experience of a legalised second marriage—a union that brings with it the wisdom of past experiences, the hope of new beginnings, and the promise of shared futures.

"*Second Chances: Navigating the Journey of legalised second marriages*" is a comprehensive guide designed to support couples embarking on this unique and rewarding path. Whether you are stepping into a legalised second marriage after the loss of a spouse, a divorce, or any other life transition, this book offers practical insights, heartfelt stories, and valuable tools to help you create a fulfilling and enduring relationship.

In legalised second marriages, couples often face a distinct set of challenges and opportunities. The blending of families, the integration of past experiences, and the establishment of new family dynamics require patience, understanding, and commitment. This book is structured to address these complexities, providing a roadmap to navigate the journey ahead with confidence and grace.

The journey begins with the **Introduction**, where we set the stage for exploring the significance of legalised second marriages. We delve into the reasons why legalised second marriages matter, highlighting their potential to bring renewed joy and fulfillment. This section emphasizes the importance of setting the stage for success by embracing change, fostering open communication, and building a strong foundation of trust and connection.

In **Embracing Change**, we discuss the crucial first step of letting go of past baggage. Acknowledging past hurts and disappointments is essential to move forward. We explore strategies for releasing resentment and regrets, cultivating self-love, and approaching your legalised second marriage with optimism and authenticity.

Communication & Connection focuses on the cornerstone of any successful relationship—effective communication. Building trust and transparency, sharing fears, hopes, and dreams, and developing active listening and empathetic communication skills are key themes in this section. We also delve into fostering emotional intimacy and creating a strong foundation of trust and understanding.

In **Blending Families**, we address the complexities of creating a unified family vision. Establishing shared values and goals, creating rituals and traditions, and navigating parenting challenges are explored in depth. This section provides practical strategies for fostering bonds with stepchildren and resolving conflicts related to parenting styles and disciplinary approaches.

Understanding Relationship Dynamics delves into the psychological aspects of relationships. We explore attachment styles and their influence on relationship dynamics, offering guidance on addressing insecure attachment patterns and fostering security. The section also covers conflict resolution skills and strengthening emotional resilience to support each other through difficult times.

Financial Fusion tackles the often challenging task of merging finances in a legalised second marriage. We discuss assessing individual financial situations, creating joint financial plans, and planning for long-term financial security. This section also provides strategies for overcoming money conflicts and communicating openly about financial priorities.

In **Cultivating Mutual Growth**, we emphasize the importance of supporting each other's personal and professional development. Encouraging continuous learning, setting shared goals and dreams, and sustaining passion and romance are key themes explored to ensure the ongoing growth and vibrancy of your relationship.

As we journey through the subsequent sections, we delve into topics such as navigating marriage laws and customs, blending families and cultures, and understanding the impact of technology and social media on relationships. Each section is enriched with quotes, case studies, practical tips, and call to action questions designed to engage and inspire you.

"Second Chances" is more than just a guide; it is a companion on your journey, offering wisdom, support, and encouragement as you navigate the complexities and joys of a legalised second marriage. Embrace the opportunity to build a strong, loving, and lasting relationship, and let this book be your trusted ally in creating a fulfilling and harmonious life together.

This revised preface provides an overview of the book's content, setting a hopeful and encouraging tone for readers as they embark on their journey of legalised second marriages.

Chapter 1
Embracing Change

Welcome to the thrilling adventure of legalised second marriages—a journey marked by the winds of change, the embrace of new beginnings, and the promise of a brighter tomorrow. In this chapter, we'll embark on a deep dive into the art of embracing change, bidding farewell to the weight of past baggage, and welcoming the dawn of a fresh chapter with open hearts and minds.

Letting Go of Past Baggage

Picture yourself on a journey to your dream destination. You meticulously pack your suitcase, carefully selecting only the essentials while leaving behind anything that weighs you down. Similarly, venturing into a legalised second marriage calls for a decluttering of the heart and mind. It's time to bid adieu to the baggage of the past—resentments, regrets, and outdated expectations—that threaten to hinder your path to happiness.

As the wise Confucius once said, "It does not matter how slowly you go as long as you do not stop." Take your time to sift through the emotional baggage, acknowledging each piece before gently releasing it. Remember, the past is but a stepping stone on the path to a brighter future.

In the words of author Paulo Coelho, "When we least expect it, life sets us a challenge to test our courage and willingness to change; at such a moment, there is no point in pretending that nothing has happened or in saying that we are not yet ready. The challenge will not wait." Embrace this challenge with courage and grace, knowing that true liberation lies in letting go.

And hey, let's sprinkle in a joke or two to lighten the mood! Why did the luggage blush? Because it saw the underwear!

Embracing New Beginnings

Now that we've shed the weight of the past, it's time to revel in the exhilarating journey of new beginnings. Think of your legalised second marriage as a blank canvas, waiting to be adorned with the vibrant strokes of love, laughter, and shared adventures. Seize the opportunity to redefine love on your own terms, crafting a narrative that celebrates authenticity and mutual growth.

As Oscar Wilde famously quipped, "To love oneself is the beginning of a lifelong romance." Embrace self-love as the cornerstone of your new beginning, nurturing your own happiness and fulfillment before intertwining your life with another. Remember, a healthy relationship with oneself lays the foundation for a harmonious union with a partner.

And speaking of new beginnings, here's a light-hearted quote to spark some inspiration: "Marriage is like a deck of cards. In the beginning, all you need is two hearts and a diamond. By the end, you wish you had a club and a spade!" Let laughter and joy be your companions on this exciting journey of love and companionship.

In conclusion, embracing change in legalised second marriages is not merely about turning a new leaf—it's about planting the seeds of resilience, authenticity, and unwavering optimism. So, dear reader, let go of the past, embrace the present, and step boldly into the future hand in hand with the one you love. After all, the best is yet to come!

Case Study: Meet Sarah and David, who found love again after experiencing the challenges of divorce. Through open communication, forgiveness, and a shared commitment to growth, they navigated the complexities of blending families and building a new life together. Their journey is a testament to the transformative power of embracing change in legalised second marriages.

Points to Remember:

Letting Go of Past Baggage:

Acknowledge and release lingering resentments, regrets, and outdated expectations from previous relationships.

Embrace the opportunity for self-reflection and personal growth that comes with letting go of the past.

Embracing New Beginnings:

Approach your legalised second marriage as a blank canvas, ready to be adorned with vibrant strokes of love and laughter.

Cultivate self-love and authenticity as the foundation for a healthy and fulfilling partnership.

Communication and Compromise:

Foster open and honest communication with your partner, building trust and understanding.

Practice patience, empathy, and compromise as you navigate the challenges and joys of blending lives together.

Call to Action: Are you ready to embrace the journey of a legalised second marriage with courage and optimism? Together, we'll navigate the twists and turns of love, laughter, and new beginnings.

Questions to Consider:

What past baggage or expectations are you ready to release in order to embrace the potential for new beginnings in your legalised second marriage?

How can you cultivate self-love and authenticity as a foundation for a healthy and fulfilling partnership?

What steps can you take to foster open communication and compromise with your partner as you navigate the challenges and joys of blending lives together?

Stay tuned for Chapter 2, where we'll delve into the art of communication in legalised second marriages. Until then, remember: love is not just a destination but a beautiful journey filled with unexpected twists and turns. Embrace it wholeheartedly.

Chapter 2
Communication and Connections

Building Trust and Transparency

In any relationship, trust and transparency form the bedrock of a strong connection. Without them, even the most compatible partners can find themselves facing misunderstandings and conflicts. Building trust involves consistent actions that demonstrate reliability, honesty, and mutual respect. Transparency means being open about your thoughts, feelings, and intentions, ensuring that there are no hidden agendas or secrets.

One of the most effective ways to build trust is through open and honest communication. This means sharing not just the good but also the difficult aspects of your life. When both partners are transparent, it fosters an environment where each person feels safe and valued. Trust isn't built overnight; it requires ongoing effort and commitment. Small, consistent acts of honesty and integrity gradually build a solid foundation of trust.

Establishing Open and Honest Communication

Open and honest communication is the key to resolving conflicts, understanding each other's needs, and maintaining a healthy relationship. This involves more than just talking; it's about listening actively, showing empathy, and being willing to understand the other person's perspective.

Active listening is a crucial component. This means fully concentrating on what your partner is saying rather than planning your response while they are speaking. It involves acknowledging their feelings, validating their experiences, and responding thoughtfully. Empathetic communication helps partners feel understood and respected, reducing the chances of misunderstandings and conflicts.

Honest communication also means being able to express your own needs, desires, and boundaries clearly and respectfully. It's important to create an environment where both partners feel safe to share their true feelings without fear of judgment or retribution. This mutual openness leads to deeper understanding and stronger emotional connections.

Sharing Fears, Hopes, and Dreams with Your Partner

Sharing your deepest fears, hopes, and dreams is an intimate act that can significantly deepen your connection with your partner. This level of vulnerability requires a high degree of trust and openness. When you share your innermost thoughts, you invite your partner into your inner world, allowing them to see and understand the real you.

Discussing your fears helps to address and overcome them together, reinforcing the idea that you are a team facing life's challenges side by side. Sharing hopes and dreams creates a shared vision for the future, aligning your goals and aspirations. This shared vision can provide direction and purpose for your relationship, making it stronger and more resilient.

By discussing these intimate aspects of your life, you also learn to support each other better. You can offer encouragement and reassurance when your partner feels insecure and celebrate together when you achieve your dreams. This mutual support strengthens the emotional bond between you, fostering a sense of unity and partnership.

Quotes:

"The best way to find out if you can trust somebody is to trust them." - Ernest Hemingway

"Communication to a relationship is like oxygen to life. Without it, it dies." - Tony Gaskins

Case Study:

Consider the case of Sarah and John, who struggled with communication early in their marriage. They decided to attend a couples' communication workshop, where they learned the importance of active listening and honest expression. By practicing these skills, they were able to rebuild trust and establish a deeper connection. Over time, they found that sharing their fears and dreams not only brought them closer but also helped them support each other more effectively.

Points to Remember:

Trust and transparency are essential for a strong relationship.

Open and honest communication involves actively speaking and listening.

Sharing your fears, hopes, and dreams fosters deeper intimacy and connection.

Building trust takes time and consistent effort.

Call to Action:

Reflect: What areas of your communication could be improved to build more trust and transparency?

Plan: Set aside regular time for open, honest conversations with your partner.

Act: Practice active listening in your next conversation, focusing entirely on your partner's words and feelings.

By prioritizing trust, transparency, and open communication, you can build a solid foundation for a strong and lasting connection with your partner.

Active Listening and Empathetic Communication

Engaging Content: Active listening and empathetic communication are vital for understanding your partner's perspective. It involves fully concentrating, understanding, responding, and remembering what is being said. This form of listening fosters empathy and respect, reducing conflicts and enhancing mutual understanding.

Quote: "Listening is an art that requires attention over talent, spirit over ego, others over self." – Dean Jackson

Case Study: Sarah and Mike found their conversations often led to arguments because they weren't truly listening to each other.

They learned about active listening techniques, such as maintaining eye contact and summarizing what the other person said before responding. Implementing these strategies helped them communicate more effectively.

Points to Remember:

Active listening involves full concentration and empathy.

Effective listening reduces misunderstandings and conflicts.

Summarizing and responding appropriately shows understanding.

Questions for Call to Action:

How can you improve your active listening skills with your partner?

What techniques can you use to show empathy during conversations?

When was the last time you felt truly listened to? How did it make you feel?

Communicating Needs and Expectations Effectively

Engaging Content: Clearly articulating your needs and expectations is essential for a fulfilling relationship. Misunderstandings often arise when assumptions are made instead of direct communication. Being clear about what you need and expect from your partner can prevent many conflicts and foster a more cooperative relationship.

Quote: "Clear communication is the key to a healthy relationship." – Unknown

Case Study: Jessica and Tom faced numerous conflicts due to unmet expectations. They attended a communication workshop where they learned to express their needs and expectations directly and respectfully. This new approach eliminated many of their misunderstandings and fostered a more harmonious relationship.

Points to Remember:

Clear communication prevents assumptions and misunderstandings.

Articulating needs directly leads to better relationship satisfaction.

Respectful expression of expectations fosters cooperation.

Questions for Call to Action:

Are there any unmet needs in your relationship that you haven't communicated?

How can you express your expectations more clearly to your partner?

What changes can you make to ensure your partner feels heard and understood?

Cultivating Emotional Intimacy

Fostering Emotional Connection and Vulnerability

Engaging Content: Emotional intimacy involves sharing your innermost thoughts and feelings, creating a space where both partners feel safe and vulnerable. This connection deepens the bond and trust between partners, leading to a more fulfilling relationship.

Quote: "Emotional intimacy is the foundation of all relationships." – Unknown

Case Study: Anna and James had a distant relationship until they started practicing daily check-ins, where they shared their highs and lows of the day. This simple act of sharing and listening helped them understand each other's emotional landscapes, fostering a deeper emotional connection and strengthening their bond.

Points to Remember:

Emotional intimacy is built on sharing and vulnerability.

Regular check-ins can deepen emotional connections.

Understanding each other's emotional state enhances bonding.

Questions for Call to Action:

How often do you and your partner share your daily experiences and emotions?

What can you do to make your partner feel more emotionally connected to you?

How can you create opportunities for deeper emotional sharing in your relationship?

Building a Strong Foundation of Trust and Understanding

Engaging Content: A strong foundation of trust and understanding is crucial for any lasting relationship. It involves consistent actions that demonstrate reliability, honesty, and integrity. Building trust requires time and effort but is essential for a healthy, enduring partnership.

Quote: "Trust is the glue of life. It's the most essential ingredient in effective communication." – Stephen R. Covey

Case Study: Monica and Daniel struggled with trust due to past betrayals. They decided to rebuild their relationship by committing to complete transparency and seeking counseling. Through these efforts, they gradually rebuilt their trust, creating a solid foundation for their relationship.

Points to Remember:

Trust is essential for effective communication and relationship longevity.

Consistent, honest actions build trust over time.

Understanding each other's values and perspectives strengthens the foundation.

Questions for Call to Action:

What actions can you take to build or rebuild trust in your relationship?

How can you demonstrate reliability and integrity to your partner?

What steps can you take to better understand your partner's perspective?

Chapter 3
Blending Families

Creating a Unified Family Vision

Blending families can be a complex and rewarding journey. Establishing a unified family vision is key to creating a cohesive and harmonious household. This vision encapsulates the collective aspirations, values, and goals of the family, providing a shared direction and purpose.

Establishing Shared Values and Goals for the Blended Family

Open Communication: "Communication is the lifeline of any relationship. When open and honest, it can bridge gaps and build strong family bonds."

Case Study: The Johnsons and the Millers blended their families and started holding weekly family meetings. This practice allowed everyone to voice their thoughts and feelings, helping them understand each other's perspectives and align their family vision.

Identify Core Values: Discuss and identify the core values that are important to each family member. Common values might include respect, honesty, kindness, and support.

Set Family Goals: Create both short-term and long-term goals that everyone can work toward. These can range from improving communication to planning family vacations or achieving personal milestones.

Point to Remember: "Goals are dreams with deadlines. Setting them together strengthens family unity."

Create a Family Mission Statement: Develop a mission statement that reflects the family's core values and goals. This statement should be a guiding principle for how the family interacts and supports each other.

Creating Rituals and Traditions to Bond as a Family Unit

Family Meals: Make it a tradition to have regular family meals where everyone sits together and shares their day.

Holiday Celebrations: Blend traditions from both sides of the family to create new, inclusive holiday celebrations.

Case Study: The Martinez family combined their Christmas and Hanukkah traditions, creating a unique, inclusive celebration that honored both parents' heritages and brought everyone closer.

Weekly Activities: Plan weekly activities such as game nights, movie nights, or outdoor adventures to foster togetherness.

Special Rituals: Establish unique family rituals, like bedtime stories for younger children or a family journal where everyone can contribute their thoughts and experiences.

Call to Action:

"What new tradition can your blended family start this week to bring everyone closer together?"

Navigating Parenting Challenges

Blended families often face unique parenting challenges, particularly when it comes to harmonizing different parenting styles and disciplinary approaches.

Addressing Parenting Styles and Disciplinary Approaches

Discuss and Align Parenting Styles: Parents should have candid conversations about their parenting philosophies and agree on a unified approach. This might require compromises to ensure consistency and fairness.

Point to Remember: "Consistency is the cornerstone of effective parenting in blended families."

Set Clear Rules and Expectations: Establish clear rules and expectations for behavior that apply to all children in the household. Consistency is key to creating a sense of stability and fairness.

Joint Decision-Making: Involve both biological and stepparents in decision-making processes regarding discipline and major life choices. This shows a united front and reinforces the family's cohesive structure.

Case Study: The Roberts family found that involving both parents in decision-making led to fewer conflicts and a more stable environment for their children.

Resolving Conflicts and Disagreements Related to Parenting

Effective Communication: Address disagreements calmly and respectfully. Use "I" statements to express feelings without blaming or criticizing.

Seek Compromise: Find a middle ground where both parents' perspectives are considered. This might involve trial and error to discover what works best for the family.

Professional Support: Consider seeking help from a family therapist or counselor if conflicts persist. Professional guidance can provide strategies for effective conflict resolution.

Call to Action:

"How can you and your partner ensure consistency in your parenting approach this week?"

Fostering Bonds with Stepchildren

Building strong relationships with stepchildren requires patience, understanding, and effort. These bonds are crucial for the emotional well-being of the children and the overall harmony of the blended family.

Building Rapport and Trust with Stepchildren

Respect Boundaries: Give stepchildren time and space to adjust to the new family dynamics. Avoid forcing relationships and let bonds develop naturally.

Quote: "Trust is built with consistency."

Show Interest: Take an interest in the stepchildren's lives, hobbies, and interests. Engage in activities they enjoy and be present in their lives.

Be Supportive: Offer support and understanding, especially during times of change or difficulty. This helps to build trust and shows that you care about their well-being.

Case Study: Sarah, a stepmother, found that by showing genuine interest in her stepdaughter's soccer games, she was able to build a strong, trusting relationship over time.

Strengthening the Parent-Stepchild Relationship Through Quality Time and Communication

One-on-One Time: Spend individual time with each stepchild to strengthen your personal bond. This can involve simple activities like going for a walk, playing a game, or having a heartfelt conversation.

Point to Remember: "Quality time is the currency of love in any relationship."

Active Listening: Practice active listening to understand the stepchildren's feelings and perspectives. Validate their emotions and experiences to foster a sense of security and trust.

ConsistentCommunication: Maintainopenandhonestcommunication. Regularly check-in with stepchildren to show that you are available and willing to listen to their concerns.

Call to Action:

"What is one activity you can do with your stepchild this week to build a stronger bond?"

By focusing on these strategies, blended families can create a nurturing and supportive environment where all members feel valued and connected. Through open communication, shared values, consistent parenting, and genuine efforts to bond with stepchildren, families can successfully navigate the challenges of blending and building lasting relationships.

Chapter 4
Understanding Relationship Dynamics

Exploring Attachment Styles

Content: Attachment styles, developed in early childhood, significantly influence how individuals relate to their partners. Recognizing your own and your partner's attachment style can help you understand relationship dynamics and work toward a more harmonious connection.

Famous Quote: "The best thing to hold onto in life is each other." – Audrey Hepburn

Case Study: *Case of Anna and Michael:* Anna had an anxious attachment style, often needing reassurance, while Michael had an avoidant attachment style, valuing independence. They attended couples therapy to understand their attachment styles and learn strategies to support each other. With time, they developed a deeper, more secure bond.

Points to Remember:

Attachment styles can be secure, anxious, avoidant, or disorganized.

Understanding each other's attachment styles can improve empathy and connection.

Therapy or counseling can be beneficial in addressing attachment-related issues.

Call to Action Questions:

What is your attachment style, and how does it influence your relationships?

How can you and your partner support each other's attachment needs?

Would exploring your attachment styles in therapy be beneficial?

Understanding How Attachment Styles Influence Relationship Dynamics

Content: Attachment styles shape how partners interact, respond to stress, and communicate. Recognizing these influences can help couples navigate challenges and foster a secure, loving relationship.

Famous Quote: "To love and be loved is to feel the sun from both sides." – David Viscott

Case Study: *Case of Brian and Lisa:* Brian's secure attachment style helped him provide stability for Lisa, who had a disorganized attachment style due to past trauma. By understanding how their attachment styles influenced their behaviors, they worked on creating a safe and predictable environment that nurtured their relationship.

Points to Remember:

Secure attachment leads to healthier relationship dynamics.

Insecure attachment can cause misunderstandings and conflicts.

Awareness and effort can transform insecure patterns into secure bonds.

Call to Action Questions:

How does your attachment style influence your reactions in stressful situations?

What steps can you take to create a more secure attachment with your partner?

How can you help your partner feel more secure in your relationship?

Addressing Insecure Attachment Patterns and Fostering Security in the Relationship

Content: Insecure attachment patterns can cause anxiety, avoidance, or inconsistency in relationships. Addressing these patterns involves building trust, enhancing communication, and creating a supportive environment.

Famous Quote: "The greatest healing therapy is friendship and love." – Hubert H. Humphrey

Case Study: *Case of Emily and David:* Emily's anxious attachment made her fearful of abandonment, while David's avoidant attachment led him to withdraw. Through couples therapy, they learned to reassure each other and create consistent, supportive interactions, fostering a secure and loving relationship.

Points to Remember:

Identify and acknowledge insecure attachment patterns.

Practice consistent and open communication.

Reassure your partner and build trust regularly.

Call to Action Questions:

What are the signs of insecure attachment in your relationship?

How can you reassure and support your partner to foster security?

What consistent actions can you take to build trust?

Managing Conflict Constructively

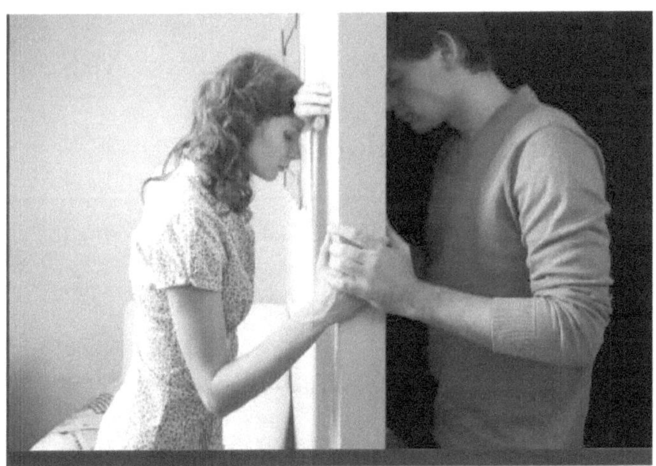

Content: Effective conflict resolution skills are essential in any marriage. Constructive management of disagreements involves empathy, respect, and a focus on resolving issues rather than winning arguments.

Famous Quote: "Conflict cannot survive without your participation." – Wayne Dyer

Case Study: *Case of Sarah and Tom:* Sarah and Tom frequently argued over finances, leading to recurring conflicts. They learned conflict resolution skills, such as active listening and "I" statements, which helped them address issues constructively. Over time, their arguments became less frequent and more productive.

Points to Remember:

Focus on the issue, not the person.

Use "I" statements to express feelings without blaming.

Listen actively and empathetically.

Call to Action Questions:

What are your current conflict resolution strategies?

How can you improve active listening during conflicts?

What steps can you take to ensure conflicts are resolved respectfully?

Developing Conflict Resolution Skills

Content: Developing conflict resolution skills involves learning to communicate effectively, understanding each other's perspectives, and finding mutually acceptable solutions.

Famous Quote: "The quality of our lives depends not on whether or not we have conflicts, but on how we respond to them." – Thomas Crum

Case Study: *Case of Jack and Laura:* Jack and Laura struggled with frequent arguments about household responsibilities. They took a conflict resolution workshop where they learned techniques like negotiation and compromise. These skills helped them reach agreements that satisfied both parties, reducing household tension.

Points to Remember:

Practice negotiation and compromise.

Focus on solutions, not problems.

Understand and validate your partner's perspective.

Call to Action Questions:

What new conflict resolution skills can you learn and apply?

How can you ensure that both partners feel heard and respected during conflicts?

What are some common conflicts you face, and how can you address them constructively?

Navigating Disagreements and Conflicts with Empathy and Respect

Content: Approaching disagreements with empathy and respect ensures that both partners feel valued and understood, leading to healthier and more productive resolutions.

Famous Quote: "Respect is how to treat everyone, not just those you want to impress." – Richard Branson

Case Study: *Case of Rachel and Kevin:* Rachel and Kevin often disagreed about parenting styles. They decided to approach these disagreements with empathy by trying to understand each other's perspectives and respecting their partner's input. This shift in approach helped them find common ground and make joint decisions.

Points to Remember:

Empathy involves understanding your partner's feelings and perspectives.

Respect is fundamental in all interactions.

Joint decision-making strengthens relationships.

Call to Action Questions:

How can you show empathy during disagreements?

What strategies can you use to ensure respect in conflicts?

How can you involve your partner in joint decision-making?

Strengthening Emotional Resilience

Content: Building emotional resilience helps couples navigate challenges and setbacks, maintaining emotional well-being and a positive relationship outlook.

Famous Quote: "Resilience is the ability to recover from setbacks, adapt well to change, and keep going in the face of adversity." – Unknown

Case Study: *Case of Megan and Josh:* Megan and Josh faced significant stress due to job losses. They focused on building emotional resilience by supporting each other, maintaining a positive outlook, and seeking professional help when needed. Their strengthened resilience helped them overcome the tough period together.

Points to Remember:

Emotional resilience involves adapting to and recovering from adversity.

Support from your partner is crucial during tough times.

Professional help can provide additional support and strategies.

Call to Action Questions:

How can you build emotional resilience individually and as a couple?

What are your strategies for supporting each other during tough times?

When should you seek professional help to strengthen your resilience?

Building Resilience to Navigate Challenges and Setbacks

Content: Resilience helps couples bounce back from challenges, maintaining a strong and positive relationship. It involves staying optimistic, flexible, and connected.

Famous Quote: "Life doesn't get easier or more forgiving; we get stronger and more resilient." – Steve Maraboli

Case Study: *The case of Alice and Brian:* Alice and Brian faced numerous setbacks, including health issues and financial struggles. They focused on staying connected and optimistic, attending resilience-building workshops together. This proactive approach helped them remain united and strong.

Points to Remember:

Stay optimistic and flexible during challenges.

Maintain strong connections with your partner.

Proactive resilience-building strengthens relationships.

Call to Action Questions:

What challenges have you faced, and how did you overcome them?

How can you stay connected and optimistic during tough times?

What resilience-building activities can you do together?

Supporting Each Other Through Difficult Times and Maintaining Emotional Well-Being

Content: Supporting each other through difficult times involves active listening, providing reassurance, and maintaining a positive outlook. It's essential for emotional well-being and a strong partnership.

Famous Quote: "True love is not about being inseparable; it's about being separated, and nothing changes." – Unknown

Case Study: *Case of Carla and Jake:* Carla and Jake went through a long-distance phase due to work commitments. They maintained their emotional connection through regular communication, virtual dates, and mutual support. This helped them stay emotionally connected despite the physical distance.

Points to Remember:

Active listening and reassurance are key.

Maintain regular and meaningful communication.

Stay positive and supportive through all challenges.

Call to Action Questions:

How do you support your partner during difficult times?

What are your strategies for maintaining emotional well-being?

How can you improve communication to stay connected?

Chapter 5
Financial Fusion

Merging Finances Successfully

Content: Successfully merging finances in a legalised second marriage requires careful assessment of individual financial situations and goals. Creating a joint financial plan and budget helps couples align their financial priorities and work toward common goals.

Famous Quote: "Financial peace isn't the acquisition of stuff. It's learning to live on less than you make so you can give money back and have money to invest. You can't win until you do this." – Dave Ramsey

Case Study: *Case of James and Linda:* James and Linda came into their legalised second marriage with different financial backgrounds. They started by assessing their individual financial situations and goals, then created a joint financial plan that included a budget, savings targets, and investment plans. This helped them work toward their shared financial future harmoniously.

Points to Remember:

Assess individual financial situations, including debts, assets, and income.

Discuss and align financial goals.

Create a joint budget that reflects both partners' priorities.

Regularly review and adjust the financial plan.

Call to Action Questions:

Have you assessed your individual financial situations and goals?

How can you create a joint financial plan that aligns with both partners' priorities?

What steps can you take to ensure regular review and adjustment of your financial plan?

Planning for Long-Term Financial Security

Content: Long-term financial security involves saving for retirement, planning for future financial goals, creating an emergency fund, and managing financial risks. Prioritizing these aspects ensures stability and peace of mind for the future.

Famous Quote: "Do not save what is left after spending, but spend what is left after saving." – Warren Buffett

Case Study: *The case of Karen and Tom:* Karen and Tom realized the importance of planning for their future after experiencing financial instability. They focused on building an emergency fund, saving for retirement, and creating a comprehensive plan for their long-term financial goals. Their proactive approach helped them achieve financial stability and security.

Points to Remember:

Start saving for retirement early and consistently.

Set clear long-term financial goals.

Create an emergency fund to cover unexpected expenses.

Manage financial risks through insurance and diversification.

Call to Action Questions:

Have you started saving for retirement and other long-term goals?

What steps can you take to build an emergency fund?

How can you manage financial risks to ensure long-term security?

Overcoming Money Conflicts

Content: Money conflicts are common in marriages, especially when merging finances. Resolving differences in financial priorities and spending habits through open communication and compromise is essential for a harmonious relationship.

Famous Quote: “A good marriage is not about how much love you have in the beginning but how much love you build till the end.” – Unknown

Case Study: *Case of David and Sarah:* David and Sarah often clashed over spending habits and financial priorities. They decided to attend financial counseling sessions, which helped them communicate openly about their concerns and find compromises. By understanding each other's perspectives, they overcame their money conflicts and strengthened their relationship.

Points to Remember:

Communicate openly and honestly about financial concerns.

Understand and respect each other's financial priorities.

Find compromises that satisfy both partners.

Consider professional financial counseling if needed.

Call to Action Questions:

What are the main sources of financial conflict in your relationship?

How can you communicate more openly about money?

What compromises can you find to resolve your financial conflicts?

Chapter 6
Cultivating Mutual Growth

Supporting Each Other's Personal Development

Content: Supporting each other's personal development is vital for a thriving relationship. Encouraging personal growth and self-improvement while providing emotional support helps both partners flourish individually and as a couple.

Famous Quote: "A great marriage is not when the 'perfect couple' comes together. It is when an imperfect couple learns to enjoy their differences." – Dave Meurer

Case Study: *Case of Alex and Maria:* Alex wanted to pursue further education, while Maria aimed to start her own business. They supported each other's aspirations by dividing household responsibilities and encouraging each other through challenges. This mutual support strengthened their bond and allowed them to achieve their personal goals.

Points to Remember:

Encourage your partner's personal growth and self-improvement.

Provide emotional support during challenging times.

Celebrate each other's achievements, big and small.

Balance personal goals with relationship commitments.

Call to Action Questions:

How can you encourage your partner's personal growth and self-improvement?

What kind of emotional support does your partner need from you?

How can you celebrate your partner's achievements together?

Setting Shared Goals and Dreams

Content: Establishing common goals and aspirations is crucial for building a united future. Planning for the future together and aligning visions ensures that both partners are working toward the same objectives, strengthening their bond.

Famous Quote: "Coming together is a beginning; keeping together is progress; working together is success." – Henry Ford

Case Study: *Case of John and Lisa:* John and Lisa sat down to discuss their long-term dreams and found that they both wanted to travel the world and eventually start a family. By setting these shared goals, they planned their finances and life decisions around these aspirations, creating a stronger partnership and a clear path forward.

Points to Remember:

Discuss and identify shared goals and dreams.

Create a plan to achieve these goals together.

Regularly revisit and adjust your plans as needed.

Celebrate milestones and progress toward your goals.

Call to Action Questions:

What are your shared goals and dreams for the future?

How can you create a plan to achieve these goals together?

How often should you revisit and adjust your plans?

Sustaining Passion and Romance

Content: Nurturing intimacy and connection is essential for sustaining passion and romance in a relationship. Keeping the romance alive through communication and quality time helps maintain a deep, loving connection between partners.

Famous Quote: "The best thing to hold onto in life is each other." – Audrey Hepburn

Case Study: *Case of Brian and Emma:* Brian and Emma found their busy schedules were impacting their intimacy. They decided to prioritize regular date nights and open communication about their needs and desires. By spending quality time together and expressing their love, they rekindled their romance and strengthened their emotional connection.

Points to Remember:

Prioritize regular quality time together.

Communicate openly about your needs and desires.

Plan special activities and surprises to keep the romance alive.

Show appreciation and affection daily.

Call to Action Questions:

How can you prioritize quality time with your partner?

In what ways can you communicate your needs and desires effectively?

What special activities or surprises can you plan to nurture romance?

Chapter 7

Navigating Marriage Laws and Customs

Understanding Hindu Marriage Laws

Content: Hindu marriage laws and customs are steeped in tradition and legal stipulations that guide the marital union. Familiarizing yourself with these requirements ensures a smooth and culturally respectful ceremony, as well as a clear understanding of the rights and responsibilities within the marriage.

Famous Quote: "Marriage is not just spiritual communion; it is also remembering to take out the trash." – Dr. Joyce Brothers

Case Study: *Case of Raj and Priya:* Raj and Priya prepared for their wedding by understanding the legal requirements and rituals of a Hindu marriage. They registered their marriage under the Hindu Marriage Act 1955, ensuring they met all legal obligations. Their awareness of their rights and responsibilities helped them navigate their marital journey with clarity and mutual respect.

Points to Remember:

Hindu marriages are governed by the Hindu Marriage Act 1955.

Legal requirements include registration, consent, and age criteria.

Traditional rituals like Saptapadi (seven steps) are integral to the ceremony.

Rights and responsibilities include mutual respect, shared duties, and legal protections.

Call to Action Questions:

Have you familiarized yourself with the Hindu Marriage Act 1955?

What traditional rituals are important to you and your partner in a Hindu marriage?

How can you ensure mutual respect and shared responsibilities in your marriage?

Likewise for other religion's laws please consult lawyers for details.

Chapter 8
Blending Families and Cultures

Creating a Unified Family Vision

Content: Blending families and cultures requires establishing shared values and goals to create a cohesive family unit. By developing rituals and traditions, families can bond and celebrate their unique blend.

Famous Quote: "Family is not an important thing, it's everything." – Michael J. Fox

Case Study: *Case of Ravi and Susan:* Ravi and Susan, both bringing children from previous marriages, focused on creating a unified family vision. They held family meetings to discuss and establish shared values, goals, and traditions, such as a weekly family game night. These efforts helped create a sense of unity and belonging within their blended family.

Points to Remember:

Discuss and agree on shared family values and goals.

Develop new family traditions that include everyone.

Celebrate cultural differences and create rituals that honor them.

Ensure all family members feel heard and valued.

Call to Action Questions:

What shared values and goals are important for your blended family?

What new traditions can you create to bond with your family?

How can you celebrate the cultural backgrounds of all family members?

Navigating Parenting Challenges

Content: Blending families often involves navigating different parenting styles and disciplinary approaches. Addressing these differences constructively is crucial for family harmony.

Famous Quote: "The way we talk to our children becomes their inner voice." – Peggy O'Mara

Case Study: *Case of Mark and Aisha:* Mark and Aisha struggled with differing parenting styles; Mark was more lenient, while Aisha was stricter. They sought the help of a family therapist to align their approaches and create a consistent discipline strategy. This helped reduce conflicts and provided a stable environment for their children.

Points to Remember:

Discuss and align parenting styles and disciplinary approaches.

Communicate openly about parenting challenges and solutions.

Seek professional help if needed to mediate differences.

Consistency in parenting helps children feel secure.

Call to Action Questions:

How do your parenting styles differ, and how can you find common ground?

What strategies can you use to resolve parenting conflicts?

Would professional guidance help in aligning your parenting approaches?

Fostering Bonds with Stepchildren

Content: Building rapport and trust with stepchildren is essential for a successful blended family. Investing in quality time and open communication helps strengthen the parent-stepchild relationship.

Famous Quote: "Children are apt to live up to what you believe of them." – Lady Bird Johnson

Case Study: *The case of Jenna and Eric:* Jenna, a stepmother to Eric's children, focused on building trust and rapport by spending one-on-one time with each child and engaging in activities they enjoyed. Over time, her efforts paid off, leading to a stronger bond and better family cohesion.

Points to Remember:

Spend quality one-on-one time with stepchildren.

Show genuine interest in their lives and interests.

Communicate openly and listen to their concerns.

Be patient and give the relationship time to develop.

Call to Action Questions:

How can you spend more quality time with your stepchildren?

What activities do your stepchildren enjoy that you can participate in together?

How can you improve communication with your stepchildren?

By focusing on these areas, Chapter 8 provides couples with practical advice and strategies for blending families and cultures. The content is designed to be engaging, informative, and motivational, helping readers create a unified family vision, navigate parenting challenges, and foster strong bonds with stepchildren.

Chapter 9
Understanding Relationship Dynamics

Exploring Attachment Styles

Content: Attachment styles play a significant role in shaping relationship dynamics. Understanding these styles helps partners recognize patterns of behavior and foster healthier connections.

Famous Quote: "The quality of your relationships is a reflection of the quality of your own internal state." – Esther Perel

Case Study: *The case of Maya and Alex:* Maya had an anxious attachment style, while Alex leaned toward avoidance. Through couples therapy, they learned to recognize and address their attachment patterns. By offering reassurance and creating a secure environment, they built a stronger, more fulfilling relationship.

Points to Remember:

Attachment styles influence how individuals perceive and respond to intimacy.

Recognizing attachment patterns promotes empathy and understanding.

Therapy or counseling can help couples navigate attachment-related challenges.

Call to Action Questions:

What is your attachment style, and how does it affect your relationship?

How can you support your partner's attachment needs?

Would exploring attachment styles in therapy benefit your relationship?

Managing Conflict Constructively

Content: Conflict is inevitable in relationships, but it's how couples manage it that determines the health of their partnership. Developing conflict resolution skills and approaching disagreements with empathy are crucial for maintaining harmony.

Famous Quote: "Conflict resolution is not about making everyone happy; it's about finding a solution everyone can live with." – Sherrilyn Kenyon

Case Study: *Case of Sam and Emily:* Sam and Emily struggled with frequent arguments about household responsibilities. They attended a conflict resolution workshop and learned communication techniques like active listening and compromise. These skills helped them resolve conflicts more effectively and strengthen their bond.

Points to Remember:

Conflict resolution skills involve active listening, empathy, and compromise.

Focus on finding solutions rather than winning arguments.

Regularly practice effective communication techniques.

Call to Action Questions:

What conflict resolution skills do you need to develop?

How can you approach disagreements with empathy and respect?

What steps can you take to improve communication during conflicts?

Strengthening Emotional Resilience

Content: Building emotional resilience is essential for navigating challenges and setbacks in relationships. Cultivating resilience helps couples support each other through difficult times and maintain emotional well-being.

Famous Quote: “Resilience is knowing that you are the only one that has the power and responsibility to pick yourself up.” – Mary Holloway

Case Study: *Case of Chris and Sarah:* Chris and Sarah faced financial hardships and health issues, but they remained resilient by leaning on each other for support. They practiced self-care, sought professional help when needed, and maintained a positive outlook, which helped them overcome obstacles together.

Points to Remember:

Emotional resilience involves adapting to and recovering from adversity.

Support from your partner is crucial during tough times.

Self-care practices promote emotional well-being.

Call to Action Questions:

How can you build emotional resilience individually and as a couple?

What strategies can you use to support each other through difficult times?

When should you seek professional help to strengthen your resilience?

By focusing on these areas, Chapter 9 provides couples with practical advice and strategies for understanding and improving relationship dynamics. The content is designed to be engaging, informative, and motivational, helping readers explore attachment styles, manage conflict constructively, and strengthen emotional resilience in their relationships.

Chapter 10

Financial Fusion

Merging Finances Successfully

Content: Successfully merging finances is crucial for a harmonious partnership. It involves assessing individual financial situations and goals and then creating a joint financial plan and budget that aligns with both partners' priorities.

Famous Quote: "Financial peace isn't the acquisition of stuff. It's learning to live on less than you make so you can give money back and have money to invest. You can't win until you do this." – Dave Ramsey

Case Study: *The case of Sarah and Mark:* Sarah and Mark came into their marriage with different financial backgrounds and goals. They sat down together, discussed their individual financial situations and aspirations, and created a joint budget that accommodated both their needs. This proactive approach helped them build a strong financial foundation for their future together.

Points to Remember:

Assess individual financial situations, including debts, assets, and income.

Discuss and prioritize financial goals as a couple.

Create a joint budget that reflects both partners' priorities.

Regularly review and adjust the financial plan as needed.

Call to Action Questions:

Have you assessed your individual financial situations and goals?

How can you create a joint financial plan that aligns with both partners' priorities?

What steps can you take to ensure regular review and adjustment of your financial plan?

Planning for Long-Term Financial Security

Content: Planning for long-term financial security involves saving for future retirement financial goals and creating an emergency fund to manage financial risks. Prioritizing these aspects ensures stability and peace of mind for the future.

Famous Quote: "Do not save what is left after spending, but spend what is left after saving." – Warren Buffett

Case Study: *Case of Emily and David:* Emily and David understood the importance of planning for their future financial security.

They committed to saving a portion of their income for retirement and set up automatic contributions to their retirement accounts. Additionally, they built an emergency fund to cover unexpected expenses, providing them with financial peace of mind.

Points to Remember:

Start saving for retirement early and consistently.

Set clear long-term financial goals and create a plan to achieve them.

Build an emergency fund to cover unexpected expenses.

Manage financial risks through insurance and diversification.

Call to Action Questions:

Have you started saving for retirement and other long-term goals?

What steps can you take to build an emergency fund?

How can you manage financial risks to ensure long-term security?

Overcoming Money Conflicts

Content: Money conflicts are common in marriages, often stemming from differences in financial priorities and spending habits. Resolving these conflicts involves open communication, understanding each other's perspectives, and finding compromises that satisfy both partners.

Famous Quote: "A good marriage is not about how much love you have in the beginning, but how much love you build till the end." – Unknown

Case Study: *Case of Jack and Sarah:* Jack and Sarah frequently argued about money, with Jack being more conservative and Sarah more liberal in her spending habits. They attended financial counseling sessions where they learned to communicate openly about their financial concerns and find compromises that allowed them to achieve their financial goals while respecting each other's values.

Points to Remember:

Communicate openly and honestly about financial concerns.

Understand and respect each other's financial priorities.

Find compromises that satisfy both partners.

Consider seeking professional help if needed to mediate differences.

Call to Action Questions:

What are the main sources of financial conflict in your relationship?

How can you communicate more openly about money?

What compromises can you find to resolve your financial conflicts?

By focusing on these areas, Chapter 10 provides couples with practical advice and strategies for achieving financial fusion in their marriage. The content is designed to be engaging, informative, and motivational, helping readers merge finances successfully, plan for long-term financial security, and overcome money conflicts in their relationships.

Chapter 11

The Importance of Emotional Intelligence in Relationships

Understanding Emotional Intelligence

Defining Emotional Intelligence (EI)

Emotional Intelligence (EI) is the ability to recognize, understand, and manage our own emotions, as well as recognize, understand, and influence the emotions of others. In relationships, especially in blended families, EI is crucial for fostering healthy interactions and resolving conflicts.

Quote: "Emotional intelligence is the key to both personal and professional success." – Daniel Goleman

Case Study: Sarah and John, both remarried with children from previous marriages, attended an EI workshop. They learned techniques to manage their emotions and understand their children's emotional needs better. This knowledge helped them navigate family conflicts more effectively.

Points to Remember:

EI involves self-awareness, self-regulation, motivation, empathy, and social skills.

High EI can lead to better communication and stronger relationships.

Developing EI requires practice and commitment.

Call to Action Question: "What steps can you take to improve your emotional intelligence starting today?"

The Role of EI in Conflict Resolution

In blended families, conflicts are inevitable. However, high EI can help resolve these conflicts constructively, ensuring that all family members feel heard and respected.

Quote: "When awareness is brought to an emotion, power is brought to your life." – Tara Meyer Robson

Case Study: The Brown family, facing constant disputes between step-siblings, utilized EI techniques such as active listening and empathetic communication. This approach reduced tensions and improved family harmony.

Points to Remember:

EI helps recognize the root causes of conflicts.

Empathy and active listening are essential components of EI.

Constructive conflict resolution strengthens family bonds.

Call to Action Question: "How can you apply emotional intelligence to resolve a current conflict in your family?"

Developing Emotional Intelligence

Self-Awareness and Self-Regulation

Understanding and managing your emotions is the first step toward high EI. This involves being aware of your emotional triggers and learning to regulate your responses.

Quote: "Self-awareness is the ability to take an honest look at your life without any attachment to it being right or wrong." – Debbie Ford

Case Study: Maria, a mother in a blended family, started journaling her emotions daily. This practice increased her self-awareness and helped her manage stress more effectively.

Points to Remember:

Regularly reflect on your emotions and their triggers.

Practice techniques such as mindfulness and deep breathing to regulate your emotions.

Understand that self-regulation is a skill that improves with practice.

Call to Action Question: "What can you do to become more aware of your emotional triggers and responses?"

Empathy and Social Skills

Empathy involves understanding and sharing the feelings of others. In blended families, showing empathy can bridge gaps and foster stronger connections.

Quote: "Empathy is seeing with the eyes of another, listening with the ears of another, and feeling with the heart of another." – Alfred Adler

Case Study: The Wilson family implemented a practice where each member took turns sharing their feelings about the week. This activity fostered empathy and improved their social skills, leading to a more supportive family environment.

Points to Remember:

Practice active listening without interrupting.

Show genuine interest in others' feelings and perspectives.

Develop social skills through positive interactions and communication.

Call to Action Question: "How can you practice empathy in your daily interactions with family members?"

Building Emotional Resilience

Emotional resilience is the ability to adapt to stressful situations and bounce back from adversity. In blended families, building resilience helps in navigating challenges more effectively.

Quote: "The greatest glory in living lies not in never falling, but in rising every time we fall." – Nelson Mandela

Case Study: After experiencing significant family upheaval, the Roberts family attended resilience-building workshops. They learned coping strategies that helped them support each other through tough times.

Points to Remember:

Develop a positive outlook and focus on solutions.

Strengthen relationships to build a support network.

Practice self-care and stress management techniques.

Call to Action Question: "What strategies can your family use to build emotional resilience together?"

Applying EI in Daily Life

Enhancing Communication

Effective communication is key to a harmonious family life. Applying EI in daily interactions can improve understanding and reduce misunderstandings.

Quote: "The way we communicate with others and with ourselves ultimately determines the quality of our lives." – Tony Robbins

Case Study: The Harris family used EI principles to enhance their communication. They practiced active listening and clear, compassionate expression of their needs and feelings, leading to fewer misunderstandings.

Points to Remember:

Use "I" statements to express your feelings without blaming others.

Listen actively and acknowledge others' feelings.

Communicate with empathy and respect.

Call to Action Question: "How can you improve communication with a specific family member using emotional intelligence?"

Fostering Positive Relationships

Strong, positive relationships are built on understanding, respect, and support. EI helps in nurturing these relationships by fostering empathy and effective communication.

Quote: "The quality of your life is the quality of your relationships." – Tony Robbins

Case Study: The Thompson family prioritized developing positive relationships through weekly family activities that promote bonding and understanding. This practice significantly strengthened their family ties.

Points to Remember:

Spend quality time together to strengthen bonds.

Show appreciation and express gratitude regularly.

Support each other's goals and interests.

Call to Action Question: "What family activity can you plan this week to strengthen your relationships?"

Managing Stress and Emotions

Effective stress and emotion management are crucial for maintaining family harmony. EI provides tools for managing stress and emotions constructively.

Quote: "You can't always control what goes on outside, but you can always control what goes on inside." – Wayne Dyer

Case Study: The Evans family adopted stress management techniques such as mindfulness and family yoga. These practices helped them manage stress and maintain a calm family environment.

Points to Remember:

Practice stress management techniques like mindfulness, exercise, and deep breathing.

Recognize and address emotional triggers.

Create a calm and supportive home environment.

Call to Action Question: "What stress management techniques can your family adopt to create a more peaceful home environment?"

Call to Action:

Question: "How can you and your family start incorporating emotional intelligence into your daily lives?"

Reflection: Identify specific areas where EI can be applied within your family. Develop a plan to enhance your EI skills together and support each other in this journey.

By embracing and developing emotional intelligence, your blended family can foster stronger relationships, resolve conflicts effectively, and create a supportive and harmonious home environment. This chapter emphasizes the significance of EI and provides practical strategies to integrate it into your family life.

Chapter 12

Health and Wellness in Blended Families

Prioritizing Physical Health

Encouraging Healthy Eating Habits

Promoting healthy eating habits is essential for the overall well-being of your blended family. This involves planning balanced meals, involving children in the cooking process, and educating them about nutrition.

Quote: "The food you eat can be either the safest and most powerful form of medicine or the slowest form of poison." – Ann Wigmore

Case Study: The Johnson family started a weekly tradition of cooking healthy meals together. They involved their children in meal planning and preparation, which not only improved their diet but also strengthened family bonds.

Points to Remember:

Plan meals that include a variety of nutrients.

Encourage children to participate in meal preparation.

Educate family members about the benefits of healthy eating.

Call to Action Question: "What new healthy dish can your family try preparing together this week?"

Promoting Physical Activity and Exercise

Regular physical activity is vital for maintaining health. Finding fun ways to stay active as a family can foster physical fitness and create lasting memories.

Quote: "Take care of your body. It's the only place you have to live." – Jim Rohn

Case Study: The Martinez family started a weekend tradition of hiking in local parks. This not only improved their physical fitness but also provided quality time together away from screens and daily stressors.

Points to Remember:

Schedule regular physical activities that everyone enjoys.

Make exercise a family affair to encourage participation.

Incorporate a variety of activities to keep things interesting.

Call to Action Question: "What family activity can you plan this weekend to get everyone moving and having fun?"

Making Health a Family Priority

Creating a family culture that prioritizes health involves setting collective goals and supporting each other in achieving them.

Quote: "Health is a state of complete physical, mental and social well-being, and not merely the absence of disease or infirmity." – World Health Organization

Case Study: The Singh family set a collective goal to reduce sugar intake and increase their daily steps. They tracked their progress together and celebrated milestones, reinforcing their commitment to a healthier lifestyle.

Points to Remember:

Set family health goals and track progress together.

Support each other's efforts to make healthier choices.

Celebrate achievements to stay motivated.

Call to Action Question: "What health goal can your family set and work toward together this month?"

Mental and Emotional Wellness

Recognizing and Addressing Mental Health Issues

Mental health is as important as physical health. Recognizing signs of mental health issues and seeking appropriate help is crucial.

Quote: "Mental health needs a great deal of attention. It's the final taboo, and it needs to be faced and dealt with." – Adam Ant

Case Study: After noticing her son's increasing anxiety, Rebecca sought help from a family therapist. This intervention helped her son develop coping strategies and improved the overall family dynamic.

Points to Remember:

Be aware of signs of mental health issues in family members.

Don't hesitate to seek professional help when needed.

Create an environment where mental health discussions are normalized.

Call to Action Question: "What steps can you take to create a more supportive environment for discussing mental health in your family?"

Promoting Open Discussions About Emotions

Encouraging open discussions about emotions helps family members feel supported and understood.

Quote: "Feelings are much like waves; we can't stop them from coming, but we can choose which one to surf." – Jonatan Mårtensson

Case Study: The Smith family established a nightly "feelings check-in" where each member shared their emotions from the day. This practice fostered empathy and understanding within the family.

Points to Remember:

Regularly check-in on each other's emotional well-being.

Encourage openness and honesty in sharing feelings.

Validate each other's emotions without judgment.

Call to Action Question: "How can you create a routine where everyone in the family feels comfortable sharing their emotions?"

Encouraging Self-Care Practices

Self-care is essential for maintaining mental and emotional health. Encouraging each family member to take time for self-care can lead to a healthier and happier family.

Quote: "Self-care is not selfish. You cannot serve from an empty vessel." – Eleanor Brown

Case Study: The Williams family set aside Sunday afternoons as "self-care time," where each member engaged in activities that rejuvenated them, such as reading, taking a walk, or practicing a hobby.

Points to Remember:

Emphasize the importance of self-care for everyone.

Support each other in finding time for self-care activities.

Respect each person's chosen self-care practices.

Call to Action Question: "What self-care activity can each family member prioritize this week?"

Building a Supportive Environment

Creating a Safe and Nurturing Home Atmosphere

A supportive home environment is one where every family member feels safe, valued, and respected.

Quote: "Home is a shelter from storms - all sorts of storms." – William J. Bennett

Case Study: The Lee family focused on creating a nurturing environment by establishing house rules based on respect and kindness. They held monthly family meetings to address any issues and reinforce these values.

Points to Remember:

Establish a set of family values centered around respect and kindness.

Create a safe space for open communication.

Regularly review and reinforce these values.

Call to Action Question: "What steps can you take to make your home a more nurturing and supportive environment for everyone?"

Encouraging Positive Relationships Among Family Members

Fostering positive relationships within the family is crucial for a supportive environment. This involves encouraging cooperation, empathy, and understanding among all members.

Quote: "Family is not an important thing. It's everything." – Michael J. Fox

Case Study: The Patel family started a tradition of weekly "gratitude circles" where each member expressed appreciation for one another. This practice strengthened their bonds and promoted positivity.

Points to Remember:

Encourage acts of kindness and appreciation within the family.

Foster a culture of empathy and understanding.

Promote cooperative activities that build positive relationships.

Call to Action Question: "How can you encourage more acts of kindness and appreciation within your family?"

Navigating Healthcare Needs

Managing Health Insurance and Medical Care

Ensuring that all family members have access to healthcare is a key component of overall wellness. This includes managing health insurance and staying on top of medical appointments.

Quote: "The greatest wealth is health." – Virgil

Case Study: The Garcia family organized their health insurance details and scheduled regular medical check-ups for all members. They used a shared calendar to keep track of appointments and health needs.

Points to Remember:

Ensure all family members have adequate health insurance coverage.

Keep a shared calendar for medical appointments.

Stay proactive about preventive care and regular check-ups.

Call to Action Question: "What steps can you take to ensure that all family members have access to regular healthcare?"

Coordinating Healthcare for All Family Members

Coordinating healthcare involves understanding the specific needs of each family member and ensuring they receive appropriate care.

Quote: "An ounce of prevention is worth a pound of cure." – Benjamin Franklin

Case Study: The Hernandez family kept detailed health records for each member, which helped them coordinate care effectively and ensure that everyone's needs were met.

Points to Remember:

Maintain up-to-date health records for each family member.

Coordinate appointments and treatments to avoid conflicts.

Be aware of each member's specific health needs and conditions.

Call to Action Question: "How can you better organize and coordinate healthcare needs within your family?"

Preparing for Medical Emergencies

Being prepared for medical emergencies is crucial. This involves having a plan in place and ensuring everyone knows what to do in case of an emergency.

Quote: "Preparedness is the ultimate confidence builder." – Vince Lombardi

Case Study: The Thompson family developed a detailed emergency plan, including first aid training for all members and a list of emergency contacts. This preparedness gave them peace of mind and readiness for unexpected situations.

Points to Remember:

Create and regularly update a family emergency plan.

Ensure all family members know basic first aid and emergency procedures.

Keep a list of emergency contacts readily available.

Call to Action Question: "What can you do to ensure your family is prepared for medical emergencies?"

Call to Action:

Question: "How can your family make health and wellness a priority starting today?"

Reflection: Discuss and set specific actions or changes that each family member can commit to enhance physical and mental wellness. Plan regular check-ins to review progress and support each other.

By prioritizing health and wellness, your blended family can create a strong foundation for a happy, balanced life. This chapter emphasizes the importance of physical health, mental and emotional wellness, and a supportive home environment, providing practical strategies to achieve these goals together.

Chapter 13
Technology and Social Media

In today's digital age, technology and social media play significant roles in our lives, influencing how we communicate, connect, and engage with the world. This chapter explores strategies for managing screen time, navigating social media responsibly, leveraging technology for connection, and addressing online conflicts.

Managing Screen Time

Setting Healthy Boundaries for Screen Use

In a world filled with digital distractions, setting boundaries for screen time is essential for maintaining balance and well-being. By establishing limits on device usage, individuals can prioritize real-life interactions and activities.

Quote: "Balance is not something you find; it's something you create." – Unknown

Case Study: The Patel family implemented a "screen-free hour" before bedtime, allowing them to unwind and connect without the distractions of technology. This simple boundary fostered deeper family bonds and improved sleep quality.

Points to Remember:

Set clear rules and guidelines for screen time within your family.

Encourage alternative activities such as outdoor play, reading, or creative pursuits.

Lead by example by practicing mindful screen usage yourself.

Call to Action Question: "What boundaries can you set to promote healthier screen habits within your family?"

Creating Tech-Free Zones and Times

Designating tech-free zones and times within the home can create opportunities for uninterrupted quality time and relaxation. By carving out spaces free from digital distractions, families can foster deeper connections and presence.

Quote: "Disconnect to reconnect." – Unknown

Case Study: The Johnson family established a "tech-free dinner table" rule, allowing them to enjoy meals together without the distraction of screens. This dedicated time for conversation and connection strengthened their family bonds.

Points to Remember:

Identify specific areas in your home where screens are prohibited, such as the dining area or bedrooms.

Designate tech-free times, such as during meals or before bedtime, to encourage face-to-face interaction.

Create alternative entertainment options, such as board games or family activities, to fill tech-free moments.

Call to Action Question: "How can you create tech-free zones and times in your home to promote quality family time?"

Encouraging Alternative Activities

Encouraging engagement in alternative activities beyond screens promotes physical, mental, and emotional well-being. By offering diverse options for recreation and leisure, families can discover new interests and hobbies together.

Quote: "The world is too big to leave it unexplored." – Unknown

Case Study: The Garcia family compiled a list of "screen-free activities" to enjoy together, including nature walks, art projects, and cooking sessions. This initiative sparked creativity and curiosity, leading to memorable shared experiences.

Points to Remember:

Brainstorm a variety of screen-free activities that appeal to different family members' interests.

Schedule regular outings or adventures to explore the outdoors and discover new places.

Encourage creativity through art, music, or DIY projects that foster self-expression.

Call to Action Question: "What alternative activities can your family explore to reduce screen time and foster creativity?"

Navigating Social Media

Teaching Responsible Social Media Use

As social media increasingly permeates daily life, teaching responsible usage habits is crucial, particularly for children and adolescents. By imparting digital literacy skills and promoting mindful engagement, families can navigate social media safely and ethically.

Quote: "With great power comes great responsibility." – Uncle Ben, Spider-Man

Case Study: The Thompson family implemented a "digital citizenship" curriculum, educating their children about online privacy, cyberbullying, and digital footprints. This proactive approach empowered their children to use social media responsibly.

Points to Remember:

Educate family members about the risks and benefits of social media use, including privacy concerns and online safety.

Establish guidelines for appropriate online behavior, such as respectful communication and critical thinking.

Foster open communication and encourage children to report any concerning or inappropriate online interactions.

Call to Action Question: "How can you teach responsible social media use within your family?"

Monitoring Online Activity and Ensuring Safety

Monitoring online activity and ensuring safety measures are in place are essential steps in protecting family members from online threats. By staying vigilant and utilizing parental controls, families can mitigate risks and promote a safer online environment.

Quote: "Safety first, even on the internet." – Unknown

Case Study: The Martinez family installed parental control software on their devices, allowing them to monitor their children's online activity and block inappropriate content. This proactive approach provided peace of mind and enhanced online safety.

Points to Remember:

Implement parental controls and privacy settings on devices and social media accounts.

Regularly review online activity and engage in conversations about internet safety with family members.

Teach children to recognize and report suspicious or harmful online behavior.

Call to Action Question: "What steps can you take to monitor online activity and ensure the safety of your family members?"

Promoting Digital Literacy

In an age of information overload, digital literacy is indispensable for navigating the online landscape effectively. By fostering critical thinking skills and media literacy, families can empower themselves to discern truth from misinformation and make informed decisions online.

Quote: "In a world where information is abundant, critical thinking is essential." – Unknown

Case Study: The Khan family engaged in regular discussions about media literacy, teaching their children to evaluate online sources critically and question the credibility of information. This proactive approach equipped their children with essential skills for navigating the digital realm.

Points to Remember:

Educate family members about the importance of critical thinking and fact-checking online information.

Encourage skepticism and curiosity, prompting family members to question the authenticity of online content.

Stay informed about emerging digital trends and technologies, adapting strategies to promote digital literacy accordingly.

Call to Action Question: "How can you promote digital literacy and critical thinking skills within your family?"

Leveraging Technology for Connection

Using Technology to Stay Connected with Family Members

While technology can sometimes be a barrier to face-to-face interaction, it also offers valuable opportunities for connection, particularly with distant family members. By leveraging digital tools such as video calls and messaging apps, families can bridge geographical distances and maintain meaningful relationships.

Quote: "Distance means so little when someone means so much." – Unknown

Case Study: The Lee family utilized video calls to stay connected with relatives living abroad, scheduling regular virtual gatherings to share updates and milestones. This innovative approach fostered a sense of closeness despite the physical distance.

Points to Remember:

Explore various digital platforms and communication tools to facilitate virtual interactions with family members.

Schedule regular video calls or virtual family gatherings to maintain connections and strengthen relationships.

Encourage family members to share photos, videos, and updates via messaging apps to stay connected between calls.

Call to Action Question: "How can you leverage technology to stay connected with distant family members?"

Leveraging Apps and Tools for Family Organization

Technology can also streamline family organization and logistics, simplifying daily routines and responsibilities. By utilizing apps and digital tools for tasks such as scheduling, shopping, and meal planning, families can enhance efficiency and productivity.

Quote: "Technology is best when it brings people together

Chapter 14

Spirituality and Shared Beliefs

Spirituality forms the foundation of many families' values and beliefs, influencing how they connect with one another and navigate life's challenges. This chapter explores the significance of spirituality in family life, encouraging open dialogue, shared rituals, and mutual support on the spiritual journey.

Exploring Shared and Individual Beliefs

Discussing and Respecting Diverse Spiritual Beliefs

In a diverse world, families often encompass a range of spiritual beliefs and practices. Embracing this diversity and fostering respect for each family member's individual beliefs cultivates a supportive and inclusive familial environment.

Quote: "In diversity, there is beauty and strength." – Maya Angelou

Case Study: The Patel family, comprising members from different religious backgrounds, embraced open discussions about their diverse beliefs. This inclusive approach fostered mutual respect and deepened their understanding of one another.

Points to Remember:

Encourage open dialogue about spiritual beliefs within the family, creating a safe space for sharing and exploration.

Respect each family member's individual beliefs, refraining from judgment or criticism.

Emphasize common values and principles that unite family members, transcending religious differences.

Call to Action Question: "How can you foster respect and understanding for diverse spiritual beliefs within your family?"

Finding Common Ground and Shared Values

Amidst diverse beliefs, families often discover common ground and shared values that form the cornerstone of their spiritual journey. Identifying and celebrating these shared principles strengthens familial bonds and fosters a sense of unity.

Quote: "Unity is strength... when there is teamwork and collaboration, wonderful things can be achieved." – Mattie Stepanek

Case Study: The Johnson family, while practicing different religions, identified shared values such as compassion, gratitude, and service to others. By focusing on these shared principles, they cultivated a sense of unity and purpose within the family.

Points to Remember:

Explore shared values and principles that resonate with all family members, regardless of religious affiliation.

Create rituals and traditions that reflect these shared values, reinforcing familial unity and connection.

Emphasize the importance of empathy and understanding in navigating differences and conflicts related to spiritual beliefs.

Call to Action Question: "What shared values can your family embrace to strengthen unity and connection?"

Creating Family Rituals and Traditions

Developing Spiritual Practices Together

Family rituals and traditions provide opportunities for spiritual growth and connection, fostering a sense of belonging and continuity across generations. By developing and participating in shared spiritual practices, families deepen their bonds and cultivate a sense of identity.

Quote: "Rituals are the poetry of life; they give meaning to the passage of time." – Unknown

Case Study: The Garcia family incorporated daily meditation sessions into their routine, providing a sacred space for reflection and introspection. This shared practice not only enhanced their spiritual connection but also promoted inner peace and emotional well-being.

Points to Remember:

Establish regular rituals and practices that align with your family's spiritual beliefs and values.

Involve all family members in the development and implementation of spiritual traditions, fostering a sense of ownership and participation.

Emphasize the importance of consistency and commitment in upholding family rituals, reinforcing their significance over time.

Call to Action Question: "How can you introduce or enhance spiritual practices within your family?"

Incorporating Beliefs into Daily Life and Celebrations

Infusing spiritual beliefs into daily life and celebratory occasions reinforces their significance and relevance within the family. By integrating spirituality into everyday activities and milestone events, families create meaningful connections and memories.

Quote: "In every moment of joy or sorrow, there is an opportunity to connect with the divine." – Unknown

Case Study: The Martinez family celebrated cultural and religious festivals with traditional rituals and prayers, infusing these occasions with spiritual meaning and significance. This integration of beliefs into their daily lives strengthened their cultural identity and familial bonds.

Points to Remember:

Incorporate prayers, blessings, or spiritual readings into daily routines and family gatherings.

Celebrate religious holidays and cultural festivals with traditional rituals and customs, instilling a sense of heritage and belonging.

Encourage family members to express gratitude and reflect on spiritual teachings during moments of joy and adversity.

Call to Action Question: "How can you integrate spiritual beliefs into your family's daily life and celebrations?"

Supporting Each Other's Spiritual Journeys

Encouraging Open Dialogue About Spirituality

Open communication about spirituality fosters understanding, empathy, and support within the family. By encouraging dialogue and sharing personal experiences, family members can nurture each other's spiritual growth and development.

Quote: "In the sharing of our stories, we find connection, understanding, and healing." – Unknown

Case Study: The Khan family initiated regular "spiritual check-ins," providing a platform for family members to share their spiritual experiences, challenges, and insights. This practice of open dialogue strengthened their familial bonds and deepened their spiritual connection.

Points to Remember:

Create opportunities for family members to share their spiritual journeys, experiences, and questions in a non-judgmental environment.

Listen actively and empathetically to each other's perspectives, validating feelings and offering support.

Foster a sense of curiosity and exploration, encouraging family members to seek out resources and guidance to deepen their spiritual understanding.

Call to Action Question: "How can you create space for open dialogue and sharing about spirituality within your family?"

Respecting Individual Practices and Paths

While shared spiritual practices are valuable, it's essential to respect each family member's individual spiritual path and autonomy. By honoring diverse beliefs and practices, families cultivate a culture of acceptance, tolerance, and mutual respect.

Quote: "The beauty of spirituality lies in its diversity; there are many paths to the divine." – Unknown

Case Study: The Lee family celebrated each family member's unique spiritual journey, respecting individual practices and beliefs. This culture of acceptance and respect fostered a sense of freedom and authenticity within the family.

Points to Remember:

Embrace diversity within the family by honoring each member's spiritual beliefs, practices, and traditions.

Avoid imposing or proselytizing beliefs onto others, respecting individual autonomy and agency.

Encourage mutual learning and exploration, valuing the richness that comes from diverse spiritual perspectives.

Call to Action Question: "How can you honor and respect the diverse spiritual practices and paths within your family?"

Chapter 15

Lifelong Learning and Development

The journey of learning and personal development is a lifelong endeavor that enriches individuals and families alike. In this chapter, we explore the importance of continuous learning, career, and personal development, cultivating new skills and hobbies, and embracing change with adaptability.

Encouraging Continuous Learning

Fostering a Love for Learning in Children and Adults

Learning is a fundamental aspect of human growth and development, spanning across all stages of life. By fostering a love for learning in both children and adults, families can cultivate curiosity, resilience, and a growth mindset.

Quote: “Education is not the filling of a pail, but the lighting of a fire.” – William Butler Yeats

Case Study: The Patel family prioritized education as a lifelong pursuit, instilling a curiosity for learning in their children from a young age. This emphasis on continuous learning empowered family members to embrace new challenges and pursue personal and professional growth throughout their lives.

Points to Remember:

Create a learning-friendly environment at home by providing access to books, educational materials, and opportunities for exploration.

Lead by example by demonstrating a passion for learning and seeking out opportunities for personal growth.

Encourage curiosity, experimentation, and resilience in the face of setbacks, fostering a growth mindset in family members.

Call to Action Question: "How can you cultivate a culture of lifelong learning within your family?"

Providing Opportunities for Educational Growth

Access to quality education is essential for personal and societal development. By providing opportunities for educational growth, families can empower their members to acquire knowledge, skills, and experiences that broaden their horizons and unlock their potential.

Quote: "Education is the passport to the future, for tomorrow belongs to those who prepare for it today." – Malcolm X

Case Study: The Johnson family invested in their children's education by enrolling them in extracurricular activities, tutoring programs, and enrichment classes. This commitment to educational opportunities expanded their children's horizons and equipped them with valuable skills for the future.

Points to Remember:

Support children's academic endeavors by providing resources, guidance, and encouragement.

Explore diverse educational opportunities, including online courses, workshops, and community programs tailored to family members' interests and aspirations.

Advocate for equitable access to education and educational resources, promoting inclusivity and social justice within the family and community.

Call to Action Question: "What educational opportunities can you provide to support the growth and development of your family members?"

Supporting Career and Personal Development

Encouraging Professional Growth and Education

Career development is a lifelong journey characterized by growth, learning, and adaptation to changing circumstances. By encouraging professional growth and education, families can empower their members to pursue fulfilling careers and achieve their professional aspirations.

Quote: "The only way to do great work is to love what you do." – Steve Jobs

Case Study: The Martinez family supported each other's career aspirations by providing emotional support, financial assistance, and networking opportunities. This collaborative approach enabled family members to pursue meaningful careers aligned with their passions and values.

Points to Remember:

Foster a supportive environment for career exploration and development, celebrating achievements and milestones along the way.

Encourage family members to pursue continuing education, professional certifications, and skill development programs to enhance their career prospects.

Provide mentorship and guidance to family members navigating career transitions or challenges, offering insights and perspective based on personal experiences.

Call to Action Question: "How can you support each other's professional growth and development within your family?"

Supporting Each Other's Career Aspirations

Each family member brings unique talents, interests, and aspirations to the table, shaping their career paths and trajectories. By supporting each other's career aspirations, families can foster a culture of encouragement, empowerment, and mutual success.

Quote: "Alone we can do so little; together we can do so much." – Helen Keller

Case Study: The Lee family established a tradition of sharing career goals and aspirations during family gatherings, offering advice, feedback, and connections to support each other's endeavors. This collaborative approach strengthened their familial bonds and facilitated professional growth for all members.

Points to Remember:

Create opportunities for family members to share their career aspirations, goals, and challenges in a supportive and non-judgmental environment.

Offer practical support, such as resume reviews, interview preparation, and networking assistance, to help family members advance their careers.

Celebrate each other's professional achievements and milestones, reinforcing a culture of mutual support and encouragement within the family.

Call to Action Question: "How can you actively support each other's career aspirations and goals?"

Cultivating New Skills and Hobbies

Exploring New Interests as a Family

Exploring new skills and hobbies as a family promotes creativity, collaboration, and bonding experiences. By embarking on shared learning journeys, families can discover new passions, strengthen relationships, and create lasting memories together.

Quote: "The family that learns together, grows together." – Unknown

Case Study: The Khan family embarked on a "family hobby challenge," where each member chose a new skill or hobby to explore together. From gardening to painting to cooking, this shared learning experience fostered teamwork, creativity, and mutual support within the family.

Points to Remember:

Brainstorm a list of new skills or hobbies to explore as a family, considering each member's interests and preferences.

Schedule regular family learning sessions or outings to practice and develop new skills together.

Emphasize the process of learning and growth rather than perfection, encouraging resilience and experimentation along the way.

Call to Action Question: "What new skills or hobbies can your family explore together?"

Promoting Lifelong Skills Development

Lifelong learning extends beyond formal education to encompass a wide range of skills and competencies that contribute to personal and professional success. By promoting lifelong skills development, families equip their members with the tools and resources to navigate life's challenges and opportunities effectively.

Quote: "Skills are the currency of the future." – Unknown

Case Study: The Garcia family prioritized skills development as a family value, encouraging each member to cultivate essential life skills such as communication, problem-solving, and financial literacy. This focus on lifelong learning empowered family members to adapt and thrive in an ever-changing world.

Points to Remember:

Identify key skills and competencies that are valuable for personal and professional growth, tailoring learning opportunities to family members' needs and interests.

Integrate skill-building activities into daily routines and family gatherings, making learning a natural and enjoyable part of family life.

Provide access to resources such as books, online courses, workshops, and mentorship opportunities to support ongoing skills development.

Call to Action Question: "How can you promote lifelong skills development within your family?"

Embracing Change and Adaptability

Preparing for Life Transitions

Change is an inevitable part of life, encompassing transitions such as career changes, relocations, and family milestones. By proactively preparing for life transitions, families can navigate change with resilience, optimism, and a sense of shared purpose.

Conclusion

In the journey of a legalised second marriage, couples embark on a path both familiar and new, where resilience, growth, and love intertwine. As the saying goes, "To love and be loved is to feel the sun from both sides," capturing the reciprocity and warmth that love brings to both partners.

Every legalised second marriage is an opportunity for a fresh start, where healing and growth prevail. As Helen Rowland once said, "When you love someone, you love the whole person, just as they are and not as you would like them to be." Embracing this sentiment allows couples like Rohan and Priya to find solace in second chances, forging bonds fortified by the wisdom gleaned from past experiences.

Trust and effective communication form the bedrock of a successful marriage. Honesty, active listening, and understanding each other's perspectives are vital. As Maya Angelou famously said, "I've learned that people will forget what you said, people will forget what you did, but people will never forget how you made them feel." Couples such as Arjun and Sita, find courage in confronting past betrayals, rebuilding trust through openness and vulnerability.

Nurturing intimacy is essential for keeping the spark alive. Quality time, affection, and emotional closeness are paramount. As Mignon McLaughlin said, "A successful marriage requires falling in love many times, always with the same person." Couples, like Vikram and Radha, exemplify this by finding joy in everyday romance, celebrating the love that grows with each passing day.

Understanding attachment styles, conflict resolution, and emotional resilience is crucial. Facing challenges together strengthens bonds. As the saying goes, "A smooth sea never made a skilled sailor." Couples such as Hari and Gita draw strength from vulnerability and communication, fostering a shared commitment to growth.

Merging finances successfully requires open discussions and collaborative decision-making. Saving for the future and aligning financial goals are paramount. As Dave Ramsey famously said, "A budget is telling your money where to go instead of wondering where it went." Couples like Sanjay and Meera exemplify the power of collaboration and shared financial goals.

Supporting personal development and sustaining passion are vital for mutual growth. A shared vision for the future strengthens bonds. As Antoine de Saint-Exupéry said, "Love does not consist in gazing at each other, but in looking outward together in the same direction." Couples such as Rahul and Ananya embody partnership, resilience, and unwavering commitment to each other's happiness.

Respecting legal requirements and cultural traditions is essential. Inclusivity and celebration of diversity are key. As Paulo Coelho said, "When you repeat a mistake, it is not a mistake anymore; it is a decision." Couples like Aakash and Devika embrace diverse traditions, ensuring their union is celebrated in accordance with their values.

Unity and inclusivity are central to blending families and cultures. Empathy, communication, and mutual respect foster harmonious relationships. As Desmond Tutu said, "You don't choose your family. They are God's gift to you, as you are to them." Couples such as Rajiv and Naina create loving and supportive environments, celebrating the richness of diversity within their families.

In conclusion, the journey of a legalised second marriage is a testament to resilience, growth, and unwavering commitment.

Through each step, couples forge bonds, overcome challenges, and build a foundation for lasting happiness together. As they embrace their unique journey, they create a blueprint for love that withstands the test of time.

www.ingramcontent.com/pod-product-compliance
Lightning Source LLC
LaVergne TN
LVHW041117150826
845673LV00007B/2089

9798894751382